MOVIE FAVORITES

Solos and Band Arrangements
Correlated with Essential Elements Band Method

Arranged by
MICHAEL SWEENEY

Welcome to Essential Elements Movie Favorites! There are two versions of each selection in this versatile book. The SOLO version appears on the left-hand page of your book. The FULL BAND arrangement appears on the right-hand page. Optional accompaniment recordings are available separately in CD or cassette format. Use these recordings when playing solos for friends and family.

ISBN 978-0-7935-5965-7

HAL•LEONARD®
CORPORATION
7777 W. BLUEMOUND RD. P.O. BOX 13819 MILWAUKEE, WI 53213

From The Universal Motion Picture JURASSIC PARK

Theme From "JURASSIC PARK"

TUBA
Solo

Composed by JOHN WILLIAMS
Arranged by MICHAEL SWEENEY

MCA music publishing

Theme From "JURASSIC PARK"

From The Universal Motion Picture JURASSIC PARK

Composed by **JOHN WILLIAMS**
Arranged by **MICHAEL SWEENEY**

TUBA
Band Arrangement

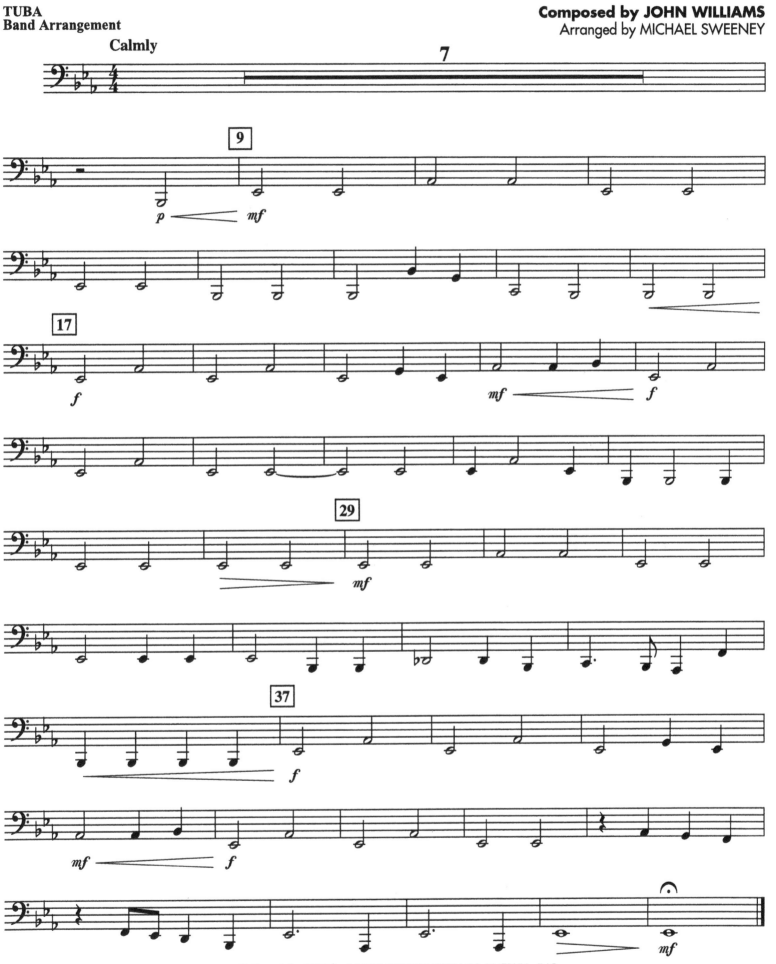

MCA music publishing

From CHARIOTS OF FIRE

CHARIOTS OF FIRE

TUBA
Solo

Music by VANGELIS
Arranged by MICHAEL SWEENEY

00860021

CHARIOTS OF FIRE

TUBA
Band Arrangement

Music by **VANGELIS**
Arranged by MICHAEL SWEENEY

From THE MAN FROM SNOWY RIVER

THE MAN FROM SNOWY RIVER
(Main Title Theme)

By BRUCE ROWLAND
Arranged by MICHAEL SWEENEY

TUBA
Solo

From THE MAN FROM SNOWY RIVER

THE MAN FROM SNOWY RIVER
(Main Title Theme)

TUBA
Band Arrangement

By BRUCE ROWLAND
Arranged by MICHAEL SWEENEY

00860021

From The Paramount Motion Picture FORREST GUMP

FORREST GUMP - MAIN TITLE
(Feather Theme)

Music by ALAN SILVESTRI
Arranged by MICHAEL SWEENEY

TUBA
Solo

From The Paramount Motion Picture FORREST GUMP

FORREST GUMP - MAIN TITLE

(Feather Theme)

TUBA
Band Arrangement

Music by ALAN SILVESTRI
Arranged by MICHAEL SWEENEY

00860021

From AN AMERICAN TAIL

SOMEWHERE OUT THERE

**Words and Music by JAMES HORNER,
BARRY MANN and CYNTHIA WEIL**

Arranged by MICHAEL SWEENEY

TUBA
Solo

00860021

MCA music publishing

SOMEWHERE OUT THERE

From AN AMERICAN TAIL

Words and Music by JAMES HORNER,
BARRY MANN and CYNTHIA WEIL

Arranged by MICHAEL SWEENEY

TUBA
Band Arrangement

Moderately Slow

MCA music publishing

00860021

From DANCES WITH WOLVES

THE JOHN DUNBAR THEME

By JOHN BARRY
Arranged by MICHAEL SWEENEY

TUBA
Solo

From DANCES WITH WOLVES
THE JOHN DUNBAR THEME

TUBA
Band Arrangement

By JOHN BARRY
Arranged by MICHAEL SWEENEY

00860021

From The Paramount Motion Picture RAIDERS OF THE LOST ARK

RAIDERS MARCH

By JOHN WILLIAMS
Arranged by MICHAEL SWEENEY

TUBA
Solo

00860021

RAIDERS MARCH

TUBA
Band Arrangement

By JOHN WILLIAMS
Arranged by MICHAEL SWEENEY

00860021

From APOLLO 13
APOLLO 13
(End Credits)

By JAMES HORNER
Arranged by MICHAEL SWEENEY

TUBA
Solo

MCA music publishing

From APOLLO 13
APOLLO 13
(End Credits)

TUBA
Band Arrangement

By JAMES HORNER
Arranged by MICHAEL SWEENEY

00860021

MCA music publishing

From The Universal Picture E.T. (THE EXTRA-TERRESTRIAL)

THEME FROM E.T. (THE EXTRA-TERRESTRIAL)

TUBA
Solo

Music by JOHN WILLIAMS
Arranged by MICHAEL SWEENEY

00860021

MCA music publishing

THEME FROM E.T. (THE EXTRA-TERRESTRIAL)

Music by JOHN WILLIAMS
Arranged by **MICHAEL SWEENEY**

TUBA
Band Arrangement

00860021

MCA music publishing

Theme From The Paramount Picture STAR TREK

STAR TREK®-THE MOTION PICTURE

TUBA
Solo

Music by JERRY GOLDSMITH
Arranged by MICHAEL SWEENEY

STAR TREK®-THE MOTION PICTURE

TUBA
Band Arrangement

Music by JERRY GOLDSMITH
Arranged by MICHAEL SWEENEY

00860021

From The Universal Motion Picture BACK TO THE FUTURE

BACK TO THE FUTURE

TUBA
Solo

By ALAN SILVESTRI
Arranged by MICHAEL SWEENEY

MCA music publishing

BACK TO THE FUTURE

From The Universal Motion Picture BACK TO THE FUTURE

TUBA
Band Arrangement

By ALAN SILVESTRI
Arranged by MICHAEL SWEENEY

MCA music publishing

00860021